YOU ARE NOT ALONE

Conquer Loneliness, Find Joy Within, Make True Friendships, & Lead a Healthier, Happier Life

Raymond Davis

Table Of Content

Introduction

"People are lonely because they build walls instead of bridges" - Joseph F. Newton

While the rooftop bar was illuminated by fairy lights, Annabelle was unnerved by a cold feeling that didn't stem from the night time temperature. Around her, muttering and laughter erupted. She felt completely invisible despite being surrounded by people, a sea of humanly figures, and lively discussions.

It had been earlier that day when she received a generic birthday card in the mail, saying "Happy Birthday", the context which seems to be more of a method of mocking her, rubbing it in her face that she has no close connection. Her year of hopping between friend groups and never quite feeling like she belonged was brought to light by the sharp reminder that no one had bothered to send her a personal message.

Her smile was forced as she awkwardly hovered around this party hosted by a friend. She was frequently bumped into and ignored by others who brushed by her or gave her a quick greeting. Her sense of loneliness was growing with every forced discussion, which felt pointless and hollow.

She watched with a twinge of jealousy as several friends gathered close, their laughter exploding like a secret language she could not understand. She felt more upset and was reminded of how alone she was.

The bitter flavor of Sarah's drink matched the bitterness that was beginning to build inside her. She felt so alone, like a ghost at her own birthday celebration, in the middle of all these people.

Everyone departed quickly after the festivities, after severally feigning familiarity with people she knew nothing about, her friend who threw the party stayed to assist in supervising the cleaning service afterwards because she couldn't do it all alone. The talk they had was not at all what she had hoped for—a discourse that would ease her fears, let her heart open, and provide her solace. In a world where millions of people exist, she felt isolated.

Undoubtedly, for a few of us, this is a daily reality: we say hello to our neighbors and coworkers without engaging in conversation. Each and every day, we live that way.

Although loneliness is something that bothers us, I've realized that it can be utilized for our own greater good and when we're not looking (least expect), we'll meet someone who we'd be able to share a bond with. We'll share laughter all day, have heart to heart connections, give and receive advice and never bother about feeling isolated.

In reality, our state of loneliness could also depend on our personality and attitude to people. This is not a guarantee that an outspoken person would be sure of having someone to talk to at all times- however, the chances that people would want to be around them are high. Who are the category of people who likes being around outspoken people? My surest guess is "the listeners". The listeners do not speak much, but they like to hear the other partys' opinion, listen to gists of all sorts in a gathering— to keep them entertained or for the sake of lessons.

A jovial person would attract people to them. As creatures in general that we are (humans and animals), we're programmed to be social- that's part of our purpose in life. People coming close to us doesn't guarantee an escape from loneliness, one could be in a circle of people and still not feel connected to anyone. Our tendency to bond with people depends on our personality, if we got connected to some extent while growing up— An isolated kid might find it a bit tedious to bond when they grow up— hence they start to get lonely and socially isolated.

Being alone is not a curse or a bad sign that no one wants to associate with you; this is a fact you should keep at the back of your mind, instead it's an opportunity for you to discover yourself and bring out the potential in you.

Loneliness can be turned into solitude, subsequently you can turn your solitude into positivity.

This book provides solutions to all forms of loneliness, no matter how severe it is.

Chapter 1

The Legend of the "Strong Man"

As per Dan Doty's Every Man Project, there is immense power in the act of purposefully gathering with the goal of opening up and sharing everything you don't usually disclose. As a nature guide and filmmaker, Dan Doty saw firsthand how desperate men were to find a means to get back in touch with one another. He presents an equation that explains the degree of connectedness in males without having to deal with exponentials, roots, or anything like that. This is how the equation looks:

Vulnerability × Time = Depth of relationship

Doty thinks he can cut down on how long it takes for men to truly build friendships by making them more vulnerable. "Maybe we should go to the pub and talk about baseball before we open up a little," he suggests. Or, we might just get right to the point: this is who I am, for this to benefit me and allow me to enjoy my life and be well. We could just go there and establish meaningful ties.

Doty's objective is to have males go straight for the emotional kill in social settings. The age range of the majority of participants is 26–42 years old. In a perfect world, Doty admits, his company wouldn't have to bridge the gap in people's lives regarding connectivity and companionship. However, initiatives like Everyman are becoming more and more important in this environment for a lot of males.

Acknowledging and Expressing Emotions

Emotional expression and acknowledgement are essential for positive social interactions for several reasons:

We establish a sense of vulnerability and honesty when we communicate our emotions to other people. By being genuine, we enable others to view us as real persons, which promotes intimacy and trust. On the other hand, suppressing feelings can act as a barrier and hinder deeper communication.

We also let others have a glimpse into our inner lives when we communicate our feelings. This enables people to comprehend our viewpoints, backgrounds, and driving forces. It is with empathy that one can build more solid bonds and encourage partnerships.

An essential component of human communication is emotion. We can more successfully express our needs and desires when we acknowledge our sentiments. For instance, expressing annoyance calmly and straightforwardly can result in a fruitful conversation, but holding in your anger might cause miscommunication and animosity.

The first step in managing our emotions is acknowledging them. By being aware of our emotions, we can pick more constructive coping mechanisms for challenging feelings rather than allowing them to rule us. With appropriate responses and transparent communication, this emotional control enables us to forge greater bonds with one another.

We may more thoroughly enjoy the delight of connection when we share our emotions. Bonds can be strengthened by shared sorrow, laughter, and even constructively express anger.

The following advice will help you recognize and healthily manage your emotions:

1. Determine your feelings: Observe your feelings for a moment. Make sure you appropriately convey your feelings with words.

2. Locate a secure area where you may be yourself: Speak with a dependable friend, relative, or professional; you can also join a support group.

3. Engage in active listening by paying close attention and making an effort to comprehend others' points of view as they express their emotions.

4. Employ "I" statements: Rather than making accusations when expressing your emotions, assume responsibility by using phrases like "I feel frustrated when..."

5. Respect other people's feelings: Give them space to feel as they do, even if you don't agree with them.

Strengthening and deepening our relationships with those around us can be achieved through recognizing and healthily expressing emotions.

49.63% of adults in the UK (or 25.99 million people) said they felt lonely sometimes, often, or always in 2022.

7.1% of the population (3.83 million) in Great Britain suffers from chronic loneliness, which is defined as feeling alone "often or always."

This is an increase from 6% (3.24 million) in 2020, suggesting that the levels of loneliness observed before the pandemic have not returned.

What is loneliness?

A subjective and unwanted experience of being alone or without company is called loneliness. It occurs when our desired and actual social relationships do not match in terms of both quantity and quality.

We are all familiar with the experience of loneliness, and it is acceptable to feel lonely occasionally. However, loneliness can be detrimental to our mental health if it is severe or persistent.

Loneliness-Influencing Factors

- Not being married
- Being a widow
- Living alone
- Unemployed
- Residing in rental housing
- Possessing an ongoing medical condition or impairment

- Coming from a community of ethnic minorities
- Holding LGBTQ Identity
- Being a young person, 16 to 24 years old
- Taking care of someone

Talking about loneliness is difficult because of its stigma. People fear feeling like a burden or being judged, this is one major reason why loneliness is on the increase.

It's common to relate loneliness to hunger.

It is the absence of emotional support and the sensual delight of being with someone who loves you. If you live in a large city like Rio de Janeiro, New York, London, or elsewhere, you will realise that loneliness is a unique kind of starvation; in fact, these are the loneliest places to be lonely. When I go for a walk on a Saturday morning, I would be amazed at how active and occupied everyone appeared to be. How could they all appear to know one another?

Long-term loneliness can negatively affect our physical and emotional well-being, which has effects on both individuals and society as a whole. Long-term loneliness can set off a vicious cycle in which one finds it more difficult to connect with others, which makes one fearful of social circumstances and makes it more difficult to escape unpleasant thoughts and find joy in life.

Long-term and persistent loneliness has been linked to negative effects on well-being and health. Studies have indicated that loneliness elevates the probability of premature death and poor physical health. Additionally, loneliness has been linked to an increased risk of mental health issues, such as depression.

Positive emotional experiences, an individual's self-perception, and general life satisfaction are all components of mental wellness, which is a subset of mental health. Reduced life satisfaction, increased morbidity, and poor physical health are all linked to reduced mental wellness.

We examine the compelling connections between mental health and loneliness and provide the testimonies of those who experience loneliness on a regular or constant basis. We take into account the conditions, scenarios, and life events that may raise our vulnerability to loneliness. We also presented recent research on how the general public perceives loneliness and the people it impacts. In this book, I'll discuss common strategies used by individuals to manage their daily loneliness and discuss the need to address structural, psychological, and practical barriers to connection to lessen the negative effects of loneliness on mental health.

Social isolation and loneliness– Are they similar?

Jim just joined a new firm as an intern. He is shy and timid. While he was welcomed by the outspoken colleagues, he still finds it not comforting enough to communicate freely with them. For the first week of work, he sits at his desk, works, and eats alone during lunch. Whenever he needs to communicate with his colleagues, it's only related to work. He doesn't have any of them on his chat app nor does he have their number, so there's no interaction in an outside of work environment. He wants to have someone to connect to but doesn't seem to know how to. He is not socially isolated but he feels lonely.

Clark lives in a bustling city apartment building. He sees his neighbors often in passing, they exchange friendly greetings, and sometimes even have brief chats about the weather or local events. John, however, feels a deep sense of loneliness. He craves a closer connection, someone to share his thoughts and feelings with on a deeper level. Despite having some social interaction, John lacks the quality connection he desires.

Janet is a single mother living in a rural town. Due to her childcare responsibilities and lack of reliable transportation, she rarely leaves her house. She has minimal social interaction, even with neighbors.

While Sarah might not necessarily feel a strong sense of loneliness (she might be content with her own company), she is objectively socially isolated due to the lack of social contact.

Paul recently moved to a new city for work. He doesn't know anyone in his new environment and feels overwhelmed by the unfamiliar surroundings. He spends most of his time alone in his apartment, working remotely and lacking opportunities to connect with others. David experiences both social isolation due to the lack of social interaction and loneliness due to the desire for connection he can't fulfill.

Social isolation and loneliness are not the same thing, but they are related. The amount of relationships a person has can be used to evaluate social isolation, which is an objective lack of social contacts. It isn't always the case that someone who is socially isolated is lonely, and vice versa.

The picture above shows a man sitting alone on a bench. His posture signifies several conditions, firstly, he probably has no one around to talk to, secondly, he is in an isolated region where there is hardly any communication with other people around. So he is isolated and he feels lonely at the same time.

You can be socially isolated but not lonely.

The influence of loneliness on men's well-being is an international issue.
Mixed research has been done on how loneliness varies by gender. Studies vary in their conclusions; some claim that women experience more loneliness than males. On the other hand, the majority of experts concur that single men have higher rates of

loneliness and that specific social standards pertaining to masculinity may contribute to this loneliness. According to some preliminary studies on loneliness, men may be less inclined than women to acknowledge feeling lonely.

Research continuously shows that women have denser social networks than males do. Women are taught to cherish friendship, confide in their friends, and cultivate intimate relationships with their closest friends from an early age. Men may be reluctant to express their emotions or show weakness, even if they have a large social circle.

In contrast to (74%) women, who felt more at ease opening up to friends, men (63%) felt more at ease were surveyed in a 2018 study of rural residents. In addition, women were more likely to engage in social activities that promote camaraderie and a feeling of community, including church events.

While social isolation is a significant worry for unmarried males, research indicates that emotional loneliness holds greater significance. A 2011 study found a greater correlation between social isolation and lower life satisfaction, but emotional loneliness was even more significant. Researchers also discovered that compared to female students, male university students reported subjective symptoms of loneliness much more frequently.

Men learn from masculine social standards that weakness means vulnerability. Additionally common is homophobia. It can be quite challenging for straight, cisgender guys to extend a friendly hand to others because they fear being branded as "gay." Even with friends, males could be afraid of being judged if they show signs of weakness or seek assistance.

Male friendships among heterosexuals frequently exhibit a conceited form of masculinity, when men boast about their sexual abilities, their business success, or their independence. Men who are having relationship difficulties may find it difficult to communicate their struggles because of this culture. Not one who makes a significant investment in mutually beneficial relationships, but rather one who exploits others, is the perfect man, as it also conveys to males.

This isolation may be a generational cycle that repeats itself. Sons who display weakness or emotion may be discouraged by men. Boys may also imitate stoic behavior if they see their fathers acting in such a manner. The shame associated with having emotional ties to other males is thus passed down from generation to generation.

Most research indicates that men are more likely than women to be in committed relationships. Some loneliness may be lessened with these partners. A lot of guys do, in fact, depend on their partners as their main or only emotional support system. Men are more susceptible to loneliness as a result of broken relationships or the death of partners. Women are more at ease being single than men, according to a 2017 survey. In the UK, 61 percent of single women and 49 percent of single males said they were satisfied.

In long-term heterosexual relationships, women can support their male partners and also help them socialize by creating and maintaining social networks. Traditionally, women have been assigned more emotional labor, such as scheduling friend outings, organizing family get-togethers, sending holiday cards, and remembering birthdays. An essential social lubricant may be lost by a guy upon the death of his spouse. Losing social opportunities and friends could result from that.

Depression and loneliness

Being alone does not always indicate a mental health issue. However, loneliness and poor mental health are intimately related since they can both exacerbate one another. Meanwhile, stronger mental health is linked to social connectivity.

Loneliness can be caused by mental illness. However, loneliness has been shown to have a deleterious effect on mental health.

Loneliness can have an influence on not just our mental but also our physical health. You may learn more about how loneliness affects health by reading this.

The degree of loneliness experienced can vary. This can vary moment by moment, during various periods, and in various situations.

Although there hasn't been much research on workplace loneliness, it's crucial to take into account how much time people spend at work. Recent research revealed that:

- Nearly half of employees report feeling lonely at work occasionally, and one in ten report feeling lonely at work frequently or always.

- Recent shifts in work habits have resulted in 24% of employees working hybrid shifts and 19% of workers working from home. It doesn't appear that this has made loneliness worse, though. Many people's relationships strengthened as a result of changes in employment locations during the COVID-19 pandemic.

- Since isolation and loneliness are different, there isn't much evidence to support the idea that having greater contact with coworkers reduces loneliness at work.

Loneliness can be exacerbated by certain factors. These encompass individual attributes such as age, race, or disability, as well as situations like living alone, going through major life transitions, or relocating to a specific place. We'll go through the risk factors of loneliness in more detail.

The effects of loneliness

At times, we've all experienced loneliness. However, extended and/or extreme periods of loneliness can be detrimental to our well-being. Our health and well-being may be impacted:

A lonely person has a 26% higher chance of dying young.

Depression and other mental health problems can be more likely to occur in those who are lonely.

Research suggests that there may be a link between loneliness and mental health: 15% of those who are not chronically lonely report suffering mental anguish.
According to 62% of young people who report being alone, "feeling lonely makes them lose confidence in themselves".
Studies indicate that loneliness is linked to high blood pressure and severe stress reactions.

In the general population, loneliness is linked to "sleep inadequacy and dissatisfaction" and "poorer sleep quality" in young adults.

Additionally, it may affect how we interact with jobs and education;

- Lower educational attainment is linked to loneliness in the early stages of adolescence.
- According to 48% of young people who report being alone, loneliness makes them "less likely to want to progress in work".
- Employees who experience greater levels of loneliness tend to perform worse at work.
- Because of its combined effects on wellbeing, health, and productivity at work, a recent study estimated that the annual cost of acute loneliness is almost £9,900 per person.

Because loneliness affects employee health, carer behaviour, productivity, and voluntary staff turnover, it is estimated that companies in the UK lose £2.5 billion annually as a result of loneliness.

According to a worldwide Meta-Gallup study conducted in October of last year, nearly 25% of adults in 142 countries said they felt lonely. As with smoking and obesity, loneliness can shorten one's life, the World Health Organisation cautions. The United Kingdom is not exempt. In December, the Office for National Statistics (ONS) conducted a study and found that 28% of adult UK citizens said they experience loneliness "often," "always," or "some of the time."

Although the exact nature of the issue is unknown, wealthier nations appear to be affected. The inclination to relocate more frequently for employment or school, longer lifespans, and postponed milestones (retirement, owning a home, and raising a family) are some of the aspects that experts point to as potential causes.

The first nation to implement a loneliness policy was Britain, six years ago. The Theresa May administration gave the ONS the job of creating national indicators to gauge loneliness levels in January 2018.
It named the world's only minister for loneliness later that year (the United Arab Emirates had a "minister for happiness," but the term was allegedly too much for the cynical British public to take). Japan is

among the other nations that have done the same.

Why Loneliness Arises Especially for Single Men

Several social and cultural variables can make single men more prone to loneliness than other people, particularly in nations with comparable social pressures like the UK, Brazil, and others. Below is a summary of these variables:

Fewer Options for Male Friendship: These could be caused as a result of male to female percentage in a location. In a place where there is more female dominance, a larger percentage of working class married men, it may seem a little bit tedious for male friendships to happen because many men are busy working away, unless there are avenues for men's meet-up like sport centres, gyms or places that attract men.

Traditional Masculinity: Men are frequently expected to be stoic and self-reliant, which discourages them from expressing their feelings and vulnerability honestly. This might make it challenging for guys to establish meaningful, emotionally invested friendships.

Emphasis on Competition: Men's social encounters with each other may be viewed as rivalries rather than as chances to bond. This could make people reluctant to ask for help or open up about personal difficulties.

Reduced Opportunities for Connecting with a Wider Social Circle: Activities that are typically associated with women, such as cooking courses and book clubs, may be viewed as less manly.

Influences from Culture

The "Strong Man" Ideal: Men may feel alone and reluctant to ask for assistance due to the assumption that they should be the main breadwinners and emotionally resilient. Men who experience loneliness may think they are falling short of what society expects of them.

Emphasis on Romantic Relationships: Marrying and having romantic relationships is generally seen by society as the ultimate source of fulfillment. For single males, this attention may make loneliness worse.

Examples in Particular Nations

The reputation of the "stiff upper lip" might provide a challenge for men who want to express their feelings and ask for help. There may also be fewer opportunities for informal connections due to the collapse of traditional pubs, which are frequently social hubs.

Brazil:The "macho" culture there tends to value men's emotional control and power. Because of this, it may be challenging for men to communicate vulnerability and build intimate friendships.

Due to these circumstances, unmarried males may;

I.   Feel isolated: Difficulties expressing emotions and fewer opportunities for intimate friendships might result in social isolation.

II.   Lonely men may Hesitate to seek help: A vicious cycle of isolation may result from their fear of being viewed as weak.

III.   Feeling bad about oneself: Loneliness can cause anxiety, despair, and even physical health issues.

Good news is there are strategies for overcoming these obstacles and creating enduring social bonds.

Chapter 2

The Many Faces of Loneliness

Beyond social isolation, there is another kind of loneliness called emotional loneliness. It's the sensation of being surrounded by people but not really connecting with them on a deep, meaningful level. It's the emotional pain of feeling ignored, misinterpreted, or unnoticed.

Being emotionally isolated isn't always related to having a tiny social network. If you don't have someone with whom you can truly connect on a deeper level, you could be in a room full of people and feel completely alone.

It's the need for strong, dependable relationships in which you feel free to express your pleasures, anxieties, and vulnerabilities without fear of being judged. It's all about having emotional support and a sense of community.

Feeling that people don't really "get" you can cause emotional loneliness to set in, even if you have friends and relatives. You may experience a disconnection and feel as though you are wearing a mask all the time.

Dr. Nobel says, "[Loneliness] is defined as the gap between the social connection we want to have with others...and [the connection] we feel we actually do have. As that gap gets larger, we describe that as greater and greater loneliness."

The agony of banishment remained the most terrible punishment, short of torture or death, imposed by kings and potentates as humans evolved, troops became tribes, and civilizations became kingdoms. It is no coincidence that isolation is still the last option for punishment in many contemporary prisons.

Because social connection plays such a fundamental part in forming our intelligence, it is poetically appropriate that feeling alone might impair our capacity for clear thinking. Our human urge for social connection is so deep-rooted. Across tens of thousands of years, the human brain's cortical mantle expanded and became more interconnected due to the need to send and receive, understand, and relay more sophisticated social cues, as most neuroscientists now believe. Stated differently, our current identity and characteristics have been largely shaped by our necessity to interact with others. Therefore, it should come as no surprise that our physiological and emotional balance is regulated by the sensory experience of social interaction, which is intricately woven into who we are. Our behavior shapes the social environment, which in turn shapes our brain and hormonal processes. The social environment influences the neuronal and hormonal signals that control our behavior.

Although running is often associated with a healthy brain, research using lab rats revealed that running had a less positive effect on the brains of animals kept in social isolation. It has been demonstrated that loneliness in people can foretell how Alzheimer's disease would develop over time. Research has indicated that loneliness can modify the transcription of DNA in immune system cells.

Indices of psychological isolation

- Feeling misinterpreted or unheard in relationships all the time.

- Desiring to express your innermost ideas and emotions yet keeping them to yourself out of concern about criticism.

- Having shallow talks with shallow relationships.
- Being surrounded by people yet nevertheless experiencing a persistent emptiness or void.
- Wanting to be intimate but not knowing how to make it happen.

Several things can lead to emotional loneliness:

1. Childhood experiences: It might be challenging to build strong relationships as an adult if there is a lack of emotional connection during childhood.

2. Relationships that are not supportive:
   Being surrounded by individuals who
   are judgmental or critical might cause
   emotional isolation.

3. Life transitions: Significant life
   transitions, such as a breakup, losing
   one's job, or relocating to a new place,
   can cause social circles to collide and
   exacerbate feelings of emotional
   isolation.

4. Social anxiety: People who are afraid
   of social situations may find it difficult
   to build meaningful relationships.

It's critical to keep in mind that
experiencing emotional loneliness is

typical. The good news is that it can be addressed and deeper connections can be made.

Social Isolation

The sense of isolation brought on by a lack of social interactions or connections is known as social loneliness. It's the lack of a robust social network and the bad feelings that come with it.

This can show itself as feeling left out of social events, having few friends, or having little interaction with relatives.

Being a part of a group and having individuals you can spend time with and connect with are desires. Feelings of exclusion or invisibleness might be brought on by social loneliness.

Indicators of social isolation may include:

- Repeatedly turning down or being reluctant to accept social event invitations.
- Not having confidantes or close friends.
- Experiencing social awkwardness or discomfort.
- Difficulty striking up talks or acquiring new acquaintances
- Choosing or being forced to spend a large period alone.

Several variables that may be involved with social Isolation are:

1. Life Changes: It can be challenging to form new social circles when relocating to a new place, taking a new job, or having a child.

2. Social Anxiety: People who are afraid of rejection or social situations may find it difficult to reach out and make new friends.

3. Introversion: Although introverts value their alone time, if they don't strike a balance between social

interaction and alone time, some may become socially lonely.

4. Lack of Social Skills: It can be difficult to establish and preserve connections if one struggles with social cues or communication.

It's vital to distinguish between social loneliness and loving solitude for its own sake. Introverts, for instance, may find that being alone energises them, but they still maintain a network of friends and family that they occasionally connect with. Negative emotions and a lack of desired social engagement are the root causes of social loneliness.

The good news is that social loneliness can be avoided. By extending your social circle, you can create more meaningful relationships and a feeling of community.

Social loneliness is about the quantity of contacts, whereas emotional loneliness concentrates on the quality of the connection. Even if they don't have a close emotional bond with every member of their social circle, someone may nonetheless yearn for a wider one.

Loneliness in Existence

The depths of existential loneliness go beyond emotional or social isolation. It's a basic and philosophical sensation of being isolated from everything and everyone else in the cosmos. It struggles with the immensity of human life and the expanse of existence.

It's the understanding that, in the end, even in intimate relationships, we are alone with our experiences. Nobody is able to fully comprehend the world in the same way as us.

Doubts about the meaning of existence and our position in the universe's scheme of things can lead to existential loneliness. It's an attempt to find purpose in an apparently meaningless universe.

This sense of loneliness may be exacerbated by the realization of our own mortality and the transience of everything.

Symptoms of Isolation in Existence

- Feeling cut off from the outside world and everything within it.

- Searching for meaning in life and wondering what it all means.

- Feeling as though they are apart from other people, even while they are in partnerships.

- A Sensation of unimportance in the scheme of things.

- Fear of the unknown and death.

Potential Reasons for Existential Isolation

Life Experiences: Life events such as trauma, bereavement, or realizing one's own death can lead to existential concerns and feelings of isolation.

Philosophical Inquiry: People often wonder where they fit into the universe, and this can occasionally make them feel alone.

Modern Society: Feelings of meaninglessness and alienation can be exacerbated by the fast-paced, impersonal aspect of modern living.

There is no easy fix for existential loneliness, but it can serve as a driving force for development on a personal level and a greater comprehension of the human condition.

Here are a few strategies to tackle existential loneliness:

Investigate Meaning: Take part in pursuits that pique your interest and give you a feeling of direction. This could include voluntary activities, artistic endeavors, or spiritual exploration.

Talk to philosophers, religious leaders, or therapists who can assist you in examining these difficult issues if you want to connect with others via shared experiences.

Embrace the Mystery: There might be serenity in realizing that there may never be a final answer to some questions in life.

Transient Isolation

In contrast to the other forms of loneliness—social, emotional, and existential—transient loneliness is situational and transient. Isolation is a transient emotion that everyone encounters occasionally.

It is caused by particular circumstances or occurrences and only lasts briefly before fading. For instance, you can experience loneliness if you recently moved to a new city and haven't made any new acquaintances.

Traveling alone, starting a new job, breaking up with someone, or spending a holiday by yourself are common triggers. Having a child or starting a new career are two great occurrences that can cause temporary loneliness while you get used to the new routines and social dynamics.

Even though it's unpleasant, temporary loneliness is typically less severe and crippling than long-term loneliness.

Symptoms of Temporary Loneliness

- Feeling lonely or uncomfortable in a social situation.

- A desire for company or connection.

- A brief decline in drive or attitude.

- Missing a loved one who isn't around right now.

The good news is that experiencing temporary loneliness is common for people. It's an indication that a fundamental desire for social interaction isn't being satisfied at the time.

Here are a few strategies to deal with temporary loneliness:

1. Determine the Trigger: Addressing the core reason for your loneliness can be aided by knowing why you're feeling that way.

2. Engage Your Network: Seek out social engagement or emotional support by establishing connections with friends, family, or coworkers.

3. Take Part in Things You Enjoy: You can improve your mood and deflect loneliness by doing things that provide you joy or fulfillment.

Make self-care a priority by giving your physical and emotional health the attention they need.

You can keep temporary loneliness from becoming a more serious problem by accepting it and taking action to deal with it.

Situational Loneliness

Situational loneliness and transient loneliness are similar, although they differ slightly in terms of length and etiology. This is how they vary:

1. Longer Lasting: Unlike transient loneliness, which passes quickly, situational loneliness can persist for weeks or even months.

2. Certain circumstances: These result from certain, continuous circumstances in your life that restrict your ability to connect socially. If these circumstances are not dealt with, they may become chronic.

The following are some scenarios that may lead to situational loneliness:

1. Life Transitions: Significant life transitions such as moving to a new place for work, having a child at home,

or going through a breakup can cause disruptions to one's current social circles and require time to establish new ones.

2. Illness: Social isolation can result from medical conditions that impair mobility or necessitate frequent hospital stays.

3. Responsibilities for Caregiving: Taking care of a sick family member can take a lot of time and energy, which makes it difficult to engage with others.

4. Living in Remote places: Individuals who reside in remote places may find

it difficult to make social relationships and engage in social activities.

Situational Loneliness Symptoms

- Feeling alone because of your way of life or daily schedule.

- Missing the relationships with people you used to know.

- Having trouble growing your social network or acquiring new acquaintances.

- A chronic loneliness that does not go away easily.

Handling Situational Isolation

1. Determine the Situation: Resolving the issue requires an understanding of its underlying causes.

2. Seek Assistance from Current Networks: Stay in touch with loved ones, even if it's only virtually.

3. Discover New Social Circles: Get involved in internet forums, neighbourhood clubs, or interest-based support groups.

4. Seek Expert Assistance: A therapist can provide direction on managing social skills and loneliness.

Situational loneliness is still fleeting, but it has the potential to last longer. You may get over loneliness and create a happy social life by being proactive in addressing the underlying issue and making new friends.

Prolonged Loneliness

Unlike the transient feelings of loneliness we've covered, chronic loneliness is a continuous and extended condition of feeling alone, alone, and cut off from other people. It's a profound and sometimes incapacitating emotional state rather than merely a transient melancholy.

Features

I. Chronic loneliness is both persistent and ongoing; it doesn't go away easily. Weeks, months, or even years may pass throughout it.

II. *Pervasive Feeling*: This kind of feeling isn't just felt in certain circumstances; it's present in every part of life, especially in social settings.

III. *Deeper Effect*: Prolonged isolation can hurt one's mental and physical well-being, increasing the risk of depression, anxiety, and even physical health issues.

Indices of Prolonged Isolation

- Feeling isolated all the time, even in public places.

- Having trouble establishing and keeping close relationships.

- A feeling of emptiness or meaninglessness in life.

- Inadequate self-worth and worthlessness sentiments.

- Physical signs such as weariness, insomnia, or hunger swings.

Reasons for Prolonged Isolation

1. Social anxiety: The dread of interacting with others might keep people from making connections and putting themselves out there.

2. Lack of Social Skills: It can be difficult to establish and preserve connections if one struggles with communication or social cues.

3. Social Exclusion: Persistent loneliness can result from being shunned or barred from social groups.

4. Life Transitions: As previously discussed, if left unchecked, life

transitions such as shifting jobs, moving, or having a child can cause social disruptions and exacerbate chronic loneliness.

Fortunately, there is treatment for chronic loneliness, despite its persistence. Here are some actions to take:

1. Self-compassion: Express your emotions and treat yourself with kindness.
Seek Professional Assistance: A therapist can provide you with tools to help you cope with loneliness and form relationships.

2. Join Support Groups: Making connections with people who have experienced loneliness yourself can be reassuring and motivating.

3. Put Your Attention Into Developing Social Skills: Engage in activities that introduce you to new people and hone your communication skills.

Recall that overcoming long-term loneliness requires patience and work. You can create deeper relationships and lead a more satisfying life by exercising patience, taking initiative, and asking for help when needed.

You can discover significance and connection in an apparently uncaring environment, as well as a greater awareness of oneself, by recognising and investigating these sentiments.

Examples of The Various Ways That Different Men May Experience Different Forms of Loneliness

Social Isolation

Situation: Justin, a recent college graduate, recently relocated for his first job to a new city. At work, he finds it hard to make acquaintances because most of his coworkers are part of established social circles. Evenings are spent alone in his flat when he misses his close pals from back home and feels alone.

Feeling Alone

Scenario: Peter enjoys a prosperous career and a wide social circle. He feels unable to fully confide in any of them, though, regarding his deeper fears and anxieties. He longs for an emotional relationship that goes beyond simple hangouts with someone who can genuinely relate to him and support him.

Loneliness in Existence

Scenario: Chris, a single father, just suffered the loss of his spouse. Without his lover, he is deeply alone and wonders what life is all about. He is troubled by the enormity of the cosmos and the transience of human connection.

Momentary Isolation

Scenario: Jude is a lone tourist discovering a foreign nation. Even while he appreciates the sights and sensations, he occasionally gets lonely, especially when he witnesses couples or groups of friends having a good time together.

Situational Isolation

Scenario: Because of his busy job and childcare responsibilities, Mark, a single father working long hours, feels alone all the time. He doesn't have much time for socializing and longs for company and adult chats.

Prolonged Aloneness

Scenario: Tom is an introverted and shy man who has spent most of his life dealing with social anxiety. He stays away from social events out of fear of being rejected, which makes him lonely all the time. His effort to find meaning in life and profound sense of emptiness only serve to increase his sense of loneliness.

Cultural Factors

The "Strong Man" Ideal: Men may be reluctant to admit their loneliness in societies that place a high value on this image, even if they are lonely on a long-term basis, out of concern that doing so would indicate weakness. Their inability to connect with others who might be experiencing similar emotions or to ask for assistance may result from this.

Recall that these are merely instances and that any person may experience loneliness differently. To identify the problem and come up with answers, it is imperative to comprehend these kinds and how they could impact solitary men.

Loneliness Spectrum Quiz

Find Your Loneliness Type with the Loneliness Spectrum Quiz

You can determine what kind of loneliness you may be experiencing by taking this questionnaire. Since there are no right or incorrect responses, be truthful with yourself and select the option that most accurately describes your experience right now.

<u>Guidelines</u>

After carefully reading each sentence, choose the response (Always, Sometimes, Rarely, Never) that most accurately expresses how frequently you feel like that.

Social Isolation

1. I don't think I have a lot of close buddies or confidantes. (Always, Sometimes, Seldom, or Never)

2. I choose to spend the majority of my free time alone. (Always, Sometimes, Seldom, or Never)

3. I turn down social gathering invitations because I'm nervous or uncomfortable. (Always, Sometimes, Seldom, or Never)

4. I long for more social interactions and a wider range of acquaintances. (Always, Sometimes, Seldom, or Never)

5. I experience social exclusion or loneliness. (Always, Sometimes, Seldom, or Never)

Emotional Isolation

6. I feel like, even with close friends, I can't be who I really am. (Always, Sometimes, Seldom, or Never)

7. I find it difficult to communicate my innermost ideas and emotions to other people. (Always, Sometimes, Seldom, or Never)

8. In my relationships, there's a feeling of emptiness or separation. (Always, Sometimes, Seldom, or Never)

9. I long for a more profound emotional bond with someone who genuinely gets me. (Always / Sometimes / Rarely / Never)

10. In my relationships, I feel unheard or misinterpreted. (Always, Sometimes, Seldom, or Never)

Existential Isolation

11. I ponder the purpose of existence and my position in the cosmos. (Always, Sometimes, Seldom, or Never)

12. I get a feeling of being cut off from the outside world. (Always, Sometimes, Seldom, or Never)

13. I'm nervous about the grandeur of existence and the transience of life. (Always, Sometimes, Seldom, or Never)

14. In the big picture, I wish to feel like I belong and have a purpose. (Always, Sometimes, Seldom, or Never)

15. I'm afraid of the dark and death. (Always, Sometimes, Seldom, or Never)

Rating

Since various forms of loneliness can coexist, there is no one correct response. Review your most common responses (Always or Sometimes) for every section, though;

Social Loneliness: You may be feeling cut off from society and lacking in social ties if the majority of your responses fall into this category.

Emotional Loneliness: If the majority of your responses fall into this category, you may yearn for more emotional closeness and connection in your relationships.

Existential Loneliness: If the majority of your responses fall into this category, you may be debating existential issues such as what life's purpose is and where you fit in the cosmos.

Recall that this serves as a springboard for introspection. Speaking with a therapist or counselor if you think you might be lonely might help you investigate the underlying reasons and create plans for creating more meaningful relationships and a more fulfilled life.

Chapter 3

Difficulties Single Men Face

Loneliness's Difficulties for Single Men

Single men may encounter particular difficulties with loneliness in industrialized nations like the UK and developing nations like Brazil.

Men have historically been under pressure to be independent and stoic. Males may find it challenging to show their emotional fragility and ask other males for emotional help as a result. It could be discouraged to engage in activities like serious talk or sharing of sentiments.

Social exchanges among men can be interpreted as contests (e.g., careers, sports). In place of a spirit of unity, this could foster rivalry.

Traditional Gender Roles: Men are traditionally expected to be the primary breadwinners in the society , according to history and culture. This pressure to perform financially can limit time and energy for social connections.

Isolation at Work: Certain male-dominated occupations (e.g., construction) could lack opportunities for social bonding within the workplace.

Age: Younger males, especially students, often struggle to form solid social circles when they transfer to new situations.

A young Brazilian man working long hours to support his family could find it difficult to connect with friends owing to restricted spare time.

In a job where men predominate, it could be difficult for a British man to discover opportunities for emotional connection with coworkers.

Remember that experiences can differ and that these are generalizations.

Vulnerability in Making Connections

When it comes to expressing vulnerability and making connections, men may have a complex web of fears. Here's a summary of some important factors:

I. Fear of Rejection: One of the biggest obstacles can be the fear of rejection, whether it comes from a romantic or social source. Vulnerability is typically frowned upon by traditional masculinity, leaving men feeling vulnerable and sometimes mocked if their efforts are met with resistance.

II. Social Stigma: Men may be expected by society to be tough, independent, and emotionless. Vulnerabilities and opening up might be interpreted as signs of weakness, which can cause anxiety about being judged or labeled as "less of a man."

III. Lack of Practice: Men may not be encouraged by societal conventions to practice making connections or expressing their feelings. This may result in a lack of expertise and self-assurance when handling certain circumstances.

IV.   Performance anxiety can be brought on by the pressure to "perform" well, to be wise, witty, or informed. This is especially true while making new friends. Men may be concerned about coming across as fascinating or favorable.

V.   Past Experiences: Anxiety might persist for a long time if there have been unpleasant past experiences with vulnerability or rejection.

These worries may show up in a variety of ways:

1. Social Withdrawal: Men might avoid situations where they have to initiate connections or be vulnerable.

2. Difficulty Expressing Emotions: They might struggle to communicate their feelings or needs openly.

3. Humour as a Defense Mechanism: Humor can be used to deflect vulnerability or create distance.

4. Anger or Aggression: Anxieties can manifest as anger or aggression, pushing people away unintentionally.

It's important to remember that these anxieties are not inherent to masculinity. By acknowledging these challenges and working towards open communication, men can build stronger, more meaningful connections.

Here are some real-life stories and testimonials from single men experiencing loneliness:

"I work in construction, and it's a pretty male-dominated environment. We don't really talk about feelings or anything like that. There's this pressure to be tough and get the job done. Sometimes, after a long day, I just want to vent or talk about something that's bothering me, but I don't feel comfortable doing that with any of the guys. I end up going home alone and feeling pretty isolated." - Mark, 38, London

"Dating apps seem like the only option to meet people these days, but I swear I get rejected more times than not. It makes me feel like there's something wrong with me. I want to put myself out there and make friends, but the fear of getting shut down constantly is paralyzing." - Miguel, 25, Rio de Janeiro

"I went through a tough breakup recently and haven't really talked about it with anyone. I don't want to seem weak or burden my friends with my problems. I know I should talk to someone, but it's hard to know who to trust and how to even start the conversation." - David, 42, Tennessee, US

"I've always been more focused on my career and haven't really invested much time in friendships. Now that I'm older, I realize how important it is to have close friends. But I don't even know how to start building those kinds of relationships. Feels like everyone else already has their groups." - Eduardo, 45, Germany.

It's important to remember these are just a few examples. Loneliness can affect men of all ages and backgrounds. However, these stories highlight the specific challenges men face in different cultures and how social expectations can contribute to feelings of isolation.

Chapter 4

The Power of a Strong Social Network

Loneliness also feels a lot like depression, though the two are not the same. One study by the University of California, San Francisco, found that the majority of those who report feeling lonely are not clinically depressed, though there are overlaps. As for me, I had no chemical or pathological reason to be unhappy. I just needed to reconnect, I needed friends. This sensation diminished over time. I found a girlfriend, and I made enough friends to get by. I'm happy again.

I also realized there was an element of my predicament that had been quite specifically male. Loneliness isn't gendered, but men in particular tend to struggle to express deep feelings and form meaningful connections. Many of us find it easier to talk about gaming, politics, or sports than to admit to suffering from loneliness or feeling unwanted by people we reach out to. We don't know who to say these things to or how to say them. This is why some men flock obsessively to secular evangelists such as Joe Rogan, Jordan Peterson and Sam Harris, who fill the fraternal vacuum with rigorous examinations of the male psyche and spread their gospel through podcasts and YouTube.

Recent research confirms this. A 2017 study at the University of Oxford showed that men bond better through face-to-face contact and activities, whereas women find it much easier to hold onto an emotional connection through phone conversations. Our social structures function differently, too.

Men aren't good at talking to each other or asking for help. This may be a cliché, but it's true. Personally, I would rather walk around lost for half an hour than risk looking incompetent by asking for directions. Every girlfriend I've had has found this baffling. I need Peak District levels of comfort and familiarity to open up to another man. The majority of my friends are female because I generally find the company of women to be more relaxed and engaging. But to help me negotiate my darkest, most brutal emotions, real-life male company is essential.

What determined whether [friendships] survived with girls was whether they made the effort to talk more to each other on the phone,' said Robin Dunbar, who led the Oxford study. 'What held up [male] friendships was doing stuff together – going to a football match, going to the pub for a drink, playing five-a-side. They had to make the effort. It was a very striking sex difference.' I've only made two close male friends since leaving university, now almost 10 years ago. There have been plenty of mates, colleagues, drinking companions and holiday bromances, but no one I would call up if my life was falling apart. As men enter their forties, the situation often gets worse. Many become siloed by family life, moving to the suburbs, socializing in couples, and maintaining a solid professional network but are unable to access the kind of raw male companionship they need. And many men are far more reliant on their partners for emotional support than they'd like to admit.' How do you make male friends in your thirties and forties? How do you create those bonding experiences? It's surprisingly hard. You may meet people at work, or perhaps through a sports team. But, all too often, you come up against a barrier.

Some of the causes of modern loneliness relate to the extent to which we have strayed from our tribal, evolutionary roots. Technology is one culprit, of course. You know the theory: by linking us all together, social media has somehow managed to drive us further apart. In a study of adults aged between 19 and 32, those who reported spending more than two hours a day on social media were twice as likely to describe feeling 'left out' or isolated. Our digital ties can feel like the real thing, but they often turn out to be weak and unsatisfying – ghostly imitations of human contact.

Hyper-urbanization and the decay of traditional communities is another. So many of us are now 'bowling alone', as US political scientist Robert D Putnam put it in his book about the decline of civic life. More and more people are taking up bowling, he pointed out, but fewer and fewer are doing so in organized teams and leagues.

One of the biggest hurdles to building modern friendships is time, an increasingly rare commodity. Friendships need time like a plant needs water. A recent study published in the Journal of Social and Personal Relationships estimated that, on average, it takes about 90 hours with someone before you consider them a real friend, and 200 to become 'close'.

Offer practical tips for men to connect with other men, like joining sports teams, men's groups, or online communities with shared interests.

Building strong connections with other men takes effort, but the rewards are great. Here are some practical tips to help you break the ice and build meaningful friendships:

<u>Initiate Connections</u>

1. Find Common Ground: Look for groups or activities based on your interests. This is a great way to meet people who already share some common ground. Board game nights, sports leagues, or book clubs can be a good starting point.

2. Join Online Communities: There are online forums and groups dedicated to almost every hobby or interest imaginable. Join these to connect with like-minded people virtually and potentially transition those connections offline.

3. Be Approachable: Strike up conversations with men you meet in everyday situations. A simple "hello" at the gym or a compliment on a cool band shirt can be the first step.

4. Offer to help
Joining a club or taking a class can have similar advantages to volunteering for a cause you support: making new friends, experiencing new things, and meeting people. Not only may this reduce loneliness,

but it can also increase happiness and life satisfaction. Working with individuals who are less fortunate than you can also increase your sense of thankfulness for what you have in your own life.

5. Get a Pet

One of the numerous advantages of having a pet—especially a dog or cat—is that they can help reduce loneliness. The act of rescuing a pet combats loneliness in multiple ways by combining the positive effects of companionship and compassion.

It can foster social connections; taking your dog for a walk exposes you to a network of fellow dog walkers, and a well-groomed dog always draws attention from onlookers. Furthermore, pets offer unconditional love, which is a powerful antidote to loneliness.

6. Speak with Outsiders

Engaging in small talk with strangers or acquaintances you meet in daily life is a simple method to make connections. As evidenced by research, doing so improves our emotional and social well-being. Talk to your neighbor the next time you're out for a stroll or grab a cup of coffee. You may discover that you feel better afterwards.

Deepen Connections

1. Be a Good Listener: Show genuine interest in others and actively listen to what they have to say. Ask follow-up questions and avoid making the conversation all about yourself.

2. Be Vulnerable (Little by Little): Don't feel pressured to share everything at once. Start by sharing small things and gradually build trust. Vulnerability fosters deeper connections.

3. Organize Activities: Take the initiative to suggest get-togethers. It could be grabbing coffee, watching a game, or going on a weekend hike. Shared experiences strengthen bonds.

4. Be Consistent: Building friendships takes time and effort. Be consistent with your communication and show your friends you care by reaching out regularly.

5. Boost Current Connections: It's likely that you already have acquaintances or family relationships in your life that you could strengthen. If so, what better way to enjoy and deepen your connections than by making more calls, hanging out with pals, and doing other things?

Starting gently could be beneficial if you're having trouble finding the motivation to connect with your loved ones. Name just one family member or friend who you could reach out to for help. The knowledge that having a robust social support system is good for your mental health is also comforting.

6. Engage in self-care: Make sure you're taking care of yourself in other ways while

you're experiencing loneliness. Self-care is a good thing no matter what, but it's especially beneficial when you're depressed. In the long run, feeling better will only come from eating well, exercising, and getting adequate sleep. Bonus: For exercise and social connection, sign up for a running club or take a fitness class.

7. Keep Intense: Set up a date with yourself to help you forget about your loneliness. Do you have any unfinished home improvement projects or hobbies you've been meaning to start? Spend some time engaging in your hobbies and self-improvement to keep your thoughts engaged.

Remember, it's okay to be yourself. Don't try to be someone you're not to impress others. The right people will appreciate you for who you are.

Rejection is Normal. Don't get discouraged if someone isn't receptive. There are plenty of men out there looking for genuine connections.

Focus on Quality, Not Quantity. It's better to have a few close friends than a large group of acquaintances.

Additional Avenues where you can find men's connection includes;

1. Men's support groups: Look online or in your community for groups specifically designed for men to connect and share experiences.

2. Therapy: A therapist can provide a safe space to explore anxieties around connection and develop healthier communication skills.

By taking these steps and being open to new experiences, you can build a strong network of male friends who will enrich your life. Remember, connection is a two-way street – put yourself out there and be open to what friendships may blossom.

Men Participating in Feminine Activities

There has been a common stigma against men participating in activities typically seen as "feminine". However, if they spark joy (book clubs, cooking classes), do not hesitate to participate in them.

I took it upon myself to make an inquiry from females about the performances of men who engage in these "feminine" activities and I realized this. Men tend to do better at these things than their female counterparts. This isn't my own thinking, rather, it's what a lot of females also admitted to. I had a discussion with a hairdresser who owns a salon close to my apartment, asking her to rate her employees' performances (male and female). She said "If there's a need for me to lay off some staff, I'll pick more of the females than male, the male employees here are really good at their craft, they learn so fast, and their work ethics are favorable". What does that mean?. This is not to say that the females suck at their job, an interpretation of her statement would be that " Even though it's a feminine job, men who took it as a job were really good at it to the extent that female customers often prefer a male service to a female.

I personally know a large percentage of chefs who are experts in the culinary field and majority of them are male chefs.

So do not be affected by the stereotype about male participation in feminine activities, join a book club if you feel like, take some cooking classes, a knitting and crocheting course, a fashion designing group and bring out the best in yourself. Spike up your productivity!

Here's why men should absolutely embrace activities typically seen as "feminine" if they bring them joy:

1. Broaden Your Horizons: Trying new things, regardless of gender norms, can lead to unexpected discoveries and passions. You might find a hidden talent for baking or lose yourself in a captivating novel.

2. Expand Your Social Circle: Activities like book clubs or cooking classes can be a great way to meet new people who share similar interests. It doesn't matter your gender;

shared passions can build strong connections.

3. Combat Stress and Improve Well-Being: Activities like reading or cooking can be a fantastic way to unwind and de-stress. Taking care of your mental and emotional health is important, no matter your gender identity.

4. Challenge Stereotypes: By defying expectations and participating in these activities, you help break down outdated gender norms. This paves the way for a more inclusive society where everyone feels comfortable pursuing their interests.

Here are some specific ways to challenge the stigma:

1. Be Open and Confident: Don't be afraid to tell people about your hobbies and interests, regardless of traditional gender roles.

2. Normalize the Activity: Frame your participation in a positive light. Talk about the enjoyment you get from it and how it benefits you.

3. Find Buddies: Look for men who share similar interests and participate in these activities together. You can create a support system and normalize it for others.

Remember, there's no shame in enjoying activities typically associated with femininity. Pursue what sparks joy and fulfillment in your life. In the long run, you'll be happier and healthier, and you might inspire others to do the same.

Building Your Squad: An Exercise for Men to Combat Loneliness

Feeling isolated? You're not alone. Many men struggle to connect with others due to social norms and anxieties. This exercise, "Building Your Squad," aims to help you identify activities you enjoy and potential social connections to combat loneliness and build meaningful friendships.

Step 1: Reflect on Your Passions

Grab a pen and paper (or your favorite note-taking app) and brainstorm activities you genuinely enjoy. Don't be afraid to challenge stereotypes! Here are some prompts to get you started:

What hobbies did you enjoy as a child?

What are you curious about learning? (Cooking, photography, fashion designing etc, coding ?)

What motivated you to opt for that choice?

What activities bring you relaxation and peace? (Reading, nature walks, meditation?)

Are there any physical activities you'd like to try? (Rock climbing, hiking, sports leagues?)

Step 2: Identify Potential Connections

Now, for each activity you listed, brainstorm potential places or groups where you can connect with others who share your interests. Here are some ideas:

I. Online communities and forums: Search for online groups dedicated to your hobbies.

II. Many social media platforms also have dedicated groups.

III. Local clubs and organizations: Look for community centers, libraries, or meetup groups that offer activities related to your interests.

IV. Classes and workshops: Enroll in a cooking class, photography workshop, or any course related to your passions. This is a great way to learn and meet new people.

V. Local businesses: Cafes with book clubs, breweries with board game nights, or sporting goods stores with organized teams – explore what your local businesses offer.

<u>Step 3: Take Action!</u>

The final step is to take action! Choose one activity and one potential connection point from your list. Here are some tips to get you started:

I. Join an online group: Introduce yourself and participate in discussions.

II. Sign up for a class: Show up early and chat with classmates before or after the session.

III. Attend a local event: Strike up conversations with people who seem friendly or share your interests.

Remember, building friendships takes time and effort. Be patient, consistent, and open to new experiences. The reward? A strong support system of men who enrich your life.

Bonus Tip: Don't be afraid to ask existing friends to join you in trying a new activity. Sharing experiences can strengthen bonds and open doors to new connections.

By following these steps and embracing your unique interests, you can build a strong "squad" of friends who share your passions and support you on your journey. You deserve to feel connected and fulfilled!

Chapter 5

Mastering the Art of Connection: Communication Skills for Men

As a Man, it is observed that you often face challenges expressing emotions and building deeper connections with friends. Here's are steps to developing communication skills that foster vulnerability and strengthen your male friendships:

Acknowledge Your Emotions

I. Identify Your Feelings: The first step is recognizing your emotions. Take time to reflect on what you're feeling – frustration, sadness, excitement, etc.

II. Label Your Emotions: Don't just feel them, name them! Putting a word to your emotions helps you understand and communicate them better.

Practice Active Listening

I. Show Interest: Good communication is a two-way street. When your friend is talking, give them your full attention. Make eye contact, nod occasionally, and avoid interrupting.

II. Ask Clarifying Questions: If something is unclear, don't be afraid to ask questions. This shows you're engaged and interested in understanding their perspective.

III. Summarize and Reflect: Briefly paraphrase what you heard to ensure understanding. This shows you were listening and allows your friend to clarify any misconceptions.

<u>Express Yourself Authentically</u>

I. Use "I" Statements: Instead of accusatory statements (e.g., "You always make me feel bad"), use "I" statements to express your feelings (e.g., "I feel hurt when you..."). This reduces defensiveness and encourages open communication.

II. Focus on Your Needs: Explain how your friend's actions affect you and what you need from them (e.g., "I need some time to process this," or "I'd appreciate it if you could listen without judgment").

III. Be Clear and Direct: Avoid vague hints or expectations. Be clear about what you're feeling and what you need from your friend.

<u>Embrace Vulnerability</u>

I. Share Your Struggles: Don't be afraid to open up about your challenges and vulnerabilities. Sharing your experiences can strengthen bonds and foster empathy.

II. Celebrate Victories Together: Equally important, share your joys and successes! Celebrate each other's wins and milestones.

III. Show Appreciation: Let your friends know you value them. Express your gratitude for their presence and support in your life.

<u>Navigate Difficult Conversations</u>

I. Pick the Right Time and Place: Don't have important conversations when you're angry or upset. Choose a calm and private setting to have a productive discussion.

II. Focus on Problem-Solving: Approach difficult conversations to find solutions, not assign blame.

III. Respect Differences of Opinion: Disagreements are normal. Listen to your friend's perspective and express your own respectfully.

Remember That;

Developing these skills takes time and don't get discouraged if it feels awkward at first.

Practice active listening and express your needs in low-pressure situations.

Acknowledge your efforts and progress in communication.

Bonus Tip

Seek Inspiration: Observe men in your life who communicate effectively and learn from their examples. You can also watch movies or TV shows featuring positive male friendships.

By following these steps and practicing open communication, you can build stronger, deeper connections with your friends. Remember, vulnerability is a sign of strength, not weakness. It allows you to express your true self and create a more fulfilling social life.

Building Friendships Outside School

Building friendships with other men can be challenging, especially when a man is no longer in school. These strategies will help you build male connections with ease:

1. Join communities and organizations that foster intimacy. Churches, volunteer organizations, and support groups may offer groups specifically for men looking for closer relationships.

2. Seek friendships with men who value alternative forms of masculinity and who are willing to talk about the need for human connection.

3. Consider working to turn acquaintances into friends. Invite a social media friend who speaks out against toxic masculinity or male loneliness to an outing.

4. Take a more active role in family efforts to grow relationships. Don't rely on women to plan all social outings or reach out to others.

5. Try starting a new group or organization. Ask other dads to meet up once a month or invite acquaintances from church to start a group for men who want to grow meaningful relationships.

6. Identify any harmful beliefs you have about friendship or masculinity. Do you believe that crying indicates weakness or that real men don't need others? Work to understand where these beliefs come from and actively correct them.

7. Practice conversations with other men ahead of time. Think about questions to ask them about their lives or opinions. Consider what you hope to share about yourself.

8. Don't rely on social media as a sole or primary source of socialization. While social media can bring people together, it also relies heavily on brief interactions rather than the sustained,

meaningful connection that grows lasting friendships.

9. Model vulnerability to other men and boys. Men who see that strong men can be vulnerable may feel more comfortable being vulnerable themselves. Sons who see their fathers invest in friendships may be less reluctant to do so themselves.

10. Therapy can help many men practice and master new social skills. Men may also benefit from therapy when social anxiety impedes relationships or when loneliness is so severe that it leads to depression.

The Strength of Vulnerability

Why Emotional Honesty Matters in Male Friendships

For generations, societal norms have painted a narrow picture of masculinity, often emphasizing stoicism and emotional suppression. This can create a barrier for men to build strong, meaningful friendships. However, the truth is, that vulnerability and emotional honesty are the cornerstones of deep and lasting connections, especially between men. Here's why:

Vulnerability Fosters Trust and Intimacy

I Sharing your true self: Opening up about your emotions, fears, and dreams allows your friends to see you as a whole person, not just a stoic facade. This fosters trust and creates a safe space for genuine connection.

II. Building empathy: By sharing your vulnerabilities, you allow your friends to understand your experiences on a deeper level. This builds empathy and allows them to offer support and encouragement when they need it most.

III. Strengthening bonds: Vulnerability fosters a sense of reciprocity in a friendship. When you open up, you encourage your friends to do the same, creating a deeper bond built on mutual trust and understanding.

<u>Emotional Honesty Creates Authentic Connections</u>

I. Beyond the surface: Male friendships often revolve around shared activities or humour. While these are important, emotional honesty allows you to connect on a deeper level, beyond the surface-level topics.

II. Real conversations: Talking about your feelings, hopes, and anxieties creates a space for real conversations with your friends. These conversations are more meaningful and leave you feeling genuinely connected.

III. Supporting each other through life's challenges: Life throws curveballs. By being emotionally honest with your friends, you're creating a support system that can offer a shoulder to cry on or a voice of reason during difficult times.

<u>Vulnerability Breaks Down Societal Stigmas</u>

I. Challenging stereotypes: By being open about your emotions, you challenge the traditional notion of masculinity that discourages vulnerability. This paves the way for a more inclusive social environment where men can express themselves freely.

II. Inspiring others: When you embrace and express your vulnerability, it can inspire your friends to do the same. This creates a ripple effect, normalizing open communication and emotional honesty among men.

III. Promoting mental well-being: Suppressing emotions can lead to isolation and negative mental health consequences. Vulnerability encourages healthy emotional expression, which is crucial for overall well-being.

Overcoming the Fear of Vulnerability

You as a man might hesitate to be vulnerable due to fear of rejection, being judged, or being seen as "weak." Here are some tips to overcome that fear:

1. Practice expressing small vulnerabilities with trusted friends first. Gradually build comfort with deeper discussions.

2. Remind yourself of the positive outcomes of vulnerability, such as stronger friendships and improved emotional well-being.

3. Seek out supportive friends: Surround yourself with men who value emotional honesty and will create a safe space for you to open up.

Building Strong Male Friendships

By embracing vulnerability and emotional honesty, men can build strong, supportive friendships. These friendships offer a multitude of benefits:

I. Reduced loneliness: Strong friendships create a sense of belonging and connection, combating feelings of isolation.

II. Improved mental health: Talking about your emotions with trusted friends can be a powerful tool for managing stress and anxiety.

III. Greater self-understanding: Open communication helps you better understand yourself and your emotions.

IV. A sense of purpose and belonging: Close friendships provide a sense of purpose and belonging, which are essential for overall well-being.

Conclusion

Forget the outdated notions of masculinity. Vulnerability and emotional honesty aren't signs of weakness; they're the foundation for strong male friendships. By embracing these qualities, you as a man can create meaningful connections, support other men through life's challenges, and ultimately experience a richer, more fulfilling life. Remember, true strength lies not in suppressing emotions, but in expressing them authentically and building strong connections with the people who matter most.

Chapter 6

Finding Purpose Beyond Relationships

Romantic relationships can be wonderful, but they shouldn't define your sense of worth or purpose. Here's a wealth of activities to cultivate self-worth and fulfillment, fostering a life rich in meaning and joy, regardless of your relationship status:

<u>Invest in Personal Growth</u>

I. Learn a New Skill: Take a class in something you've always wanted to try, like photography, coding, cooking, or a new language. Mastering a new skill boosts confidence and opens doors to new hobbies and interests.

II. Read and Reflect: Dive into books on personal development, philosophy, or biographies of inspiring individuals. Reading broadens your perspective and provides valuable life lessons.

III. Start a Journal: Dedicate time to self-reflection by journaling your thoughts, feelings, and goals. This practice helps you understand yourself better and track your progress.

IV. Volunteer Your Time: Give back to your community by volunteering for a cause you care about. Helping others can be an incredibly rewarding experience that fosters a sense of purpose.

<u>Prioritize Physical and Mental Well-Being</u>

I. Develop a Fitness Routine: Exercise releases endorphins, natural mood elevators that combat stress and promote overall well-being. Find activities you enjoy, like running, swimming, team sports, or yoga.

II. Practice Mindfulness: Engage in activities that promote relaxation and self-awareness. Techniques like meditation or deep breathing can help manage stress and improve emotional clarity.

III. Fuel Your Body Right: Nourish yourself with healthy, nutritious food that gives you energy and supports your physical and mental health.

IV. Prioritize Sleep: Getting enough quality sleep is crucial for both physical and mental well-being. Establish a consistent sleep schedule and create a relaxing bedtime routine.

<u>Explore Your Passions and Interests</u>

I. Pursue Hobbies You Enjoy: Dedicate time to activities that bring you joy, like playing music, painting, playing video games, or spending time outdoors. These hobbies provide a creative outlet and a sense of accomplishment.

II. Travel and Explore: Explore new places, cultures, and experiences. Travelling broadens your horizons, creates lasting memories, and fosters a sense of adventure.

III. Connect with Nature: Spend time in nature, go for walks in the park, hike in the wilderness, or simply sit in your backyard and observe the surroundings. Immersing yourself in nature is a powerful stress reliever and can boost your mood.

Build Strong Social Connections

I. Nurture Existing Friendships: Invest time in your existing friendships. Reach out to friends, plan activities together, and offer support when needed. Strong social connections are essential for happiness and well-being.

II. Join Social Groups: Join clubs, online communities, or local meetups based on your interests. This is a great way to connect with like-minded people and build new friendships.

III. Reconnect with Old Friends: Reach out to old friends you've lost touch with. Reconnecting with people from your past can be a rewarding experience.

<u>Celebrate Your Accomplishments</u>

I. Big or Small: Take the time to acknowledge and celebrate your achievements, no matter how big or small. This reinforces your self-confidence and motivates you to keep striving for your goals.

II. Set Goals and Track Progress: Setting achievable goals for yourself provides a sense of direction and purpose. Track your progress and reward yourself for reaching milestones.

III. Practice Gratitude: Reflect on the positive aspects of your life, the people you care about, and the things you're grateful for. Gratitude fosters a positive mindset and boosts self-worth.

Remember, building self-worth and a sense of purpose is a journey, not a destination. Embrace these activities, celebrate your progress, and enjoy the process of creating a fulfilling life that you love, with or without a romantic partner.

Highlight the importance of hobbies, volunteering, or pursuing personal goals.

Include stories of single men who have found fulfillment through various passions and pursuits.

Chapter 7

Reframing Your Approach to Dating

Why Bringing a Romantic Partner Into the Gap to Combat Loneliness Can Backfire

Seeking a spouse purely to overcome loneliness can have unforeseen repercussions, even while romantic partnerships can be tremendous providers of companionship and affection. For the following reasons, prioritizing the development of a satisfying life apart from relationships is crucial.

I. Happiness Via Another: Having a spouse isn't the only way to overcome loneliness, so don't have unreasonable expectations. Loneliness cannot be magically eliminated by romantic relationships; they need work.

II. Unhealthy codependency can result from relying entirely on a partner for emotional fulfillment. Having your own happiness and feeling of purpose outside of relationships is vital.

Hazardous Attraction

I. Attracting the Wrong People: Desperately looking for a mate could cause you to ignore warning signs and end up in a toxic relationship.

II. Finding Someone Who Truly Shares Your Values and Interests may not be your first priority if you're more concerned with "filling a void" than with compatibility.

<u>Relationship Stress</u>

I. Pressure to Perform: The need to keep the relationship going to prevent loneliness can put a strain on the dynamic and cause worry in both parties.

II. Neglecting Self-Growth: Over time, resentment and discontent can result from putting your relationship above your own interests and hobbies.

<u>Trouble Forming Deeper Connections</u>

I. Genuine Self-Showing: Searching for someone to replace a gap in your life may make it more difficult for you to be genuine in a relationship.

II. Emotional baggage: Unresolved loneliness may result in emotional baggage that prevents one from developing more meaningful relationships.

Options to Fight Loneliness

1. Create lasting friendships by making time for the relationships you already have and making new ones. One effective way to combat loneliness is to maintain strong social ties.

2. Examine your interests: Follow your passions and the pursuits that make you happy and fulfill you.

3. Put self-care first: Make exercise, a good diet, adequate sleep, and relaxation methods a priority for your physical and mental well-being.

4. Seek professional assistance: If you're experiencing long-term loneliness, you might want to speak with a therapist who can offer techniques and support.

Keep in mind that when you live a fulfilling life, people who share your interests and values are drawn to you and love will find you when you least expect it.

You Become your best self by emphasizing personal development and self-improvement.

Create a supportive network of family and friends who enhance your life.

You'll be in a better position to draw in and maintain a happy, satisfying relationship when the time is right if you put your attention on your own pleasure and well-being. Your life should be made even more fulfilling by your relationship; they shouldn't be your exclusive source of joy.

Getting Around in the Dating World

Positive Attitudes and Steering Clear of Manipulation

Dating may be a thrilling experience, but it's crucial to go into it with an open mind and be cautious of any potential dangers. This is a how-to which helps you date confidently and stay away from manipulation:

<u>Well-Being Dating Habits</u>

I. Know Your Worth: Consider your ideals, your criteria for a relationship, and your deal breakers before stepping into the dating pool. You can attract compatible matches with this clarity.

II. Communicate Openly: In any relationship, communication must be honest and transparent. Straightforwardly and confidently, state your requirements, wants, and boundaries.

III. Respect Each Other's Boundaries: Honor your partner's boundaries in the same way that you set your own. Trust and respect are fostered by this.

IV. Go at Your Own Pace: Do not feel compelled to jump right into commitment or intimacy. A good relationship grows organically over time.

V. Maintain Your Independence: Maintain your interests, activities, and friendships when you're dating. This prevents co-dependency and maintains your life meaningful.

VI. Watch Out for Red Flags: Pay attention to possible warning signs such as extreme jealousy, domineering conduct, or unceasing criticism. These are not signs to disregard.

Defining Limitations

I. Determine Your Limits: Decide what actions in a relationship you will and will not accept. Boundaries about communication (such as refraining from late-night messaging) and emotions are all included in this.

II. Make Clear Communication: Tell your date exactly what your boundaries are. Express your feelings about specific behaviors using "I" statements (e.g., "I feel uncomfortable when you...").

III. Always Be Ready to Apply: Never hesitate to set and enforce boundaries. If someone consistently pushes your boundaries, it might be time to reassess the partnership.

<u>Steer clear of manipulation</u>

I. Identify Manipulative Tactics: Be mindful of typical manipulation techniques such as gaslighting, guilt-tripping, and love bombing (using excessive affection to forge a bond).

II. Trust Your Gut: Have faith in your instincts if anything seems strange or uneasy. If you sense that something is manipulating the relationship, don't be scared to end it.

III. Maintain Your Support System: If you suspect manipulation, you can talk about your dating experiences and seek unbiased counsel by having a solid support network of friends and family.

IV. Seeking professional assistance from a therapist could be beneficial if you're experiencing manipulation in your relationship.

Mutual respect, honest communication, and trust are the cornerstones of healthy relationships. It is right for you to get consideration and care. A fulfilling, healthy relationship is what you should always aim for.

The first few times you go out, meet dates in public areas. Don't divulge money or personal information too soon. Take note of your date's behavior as well as their words. It's acceptable to decline a date or stop a relationship if it doesn't feel right.

You can date with confidence if you adhere to these rules and put your health first to discover a companion who makes positive changes in your life.

Chapter 8

Overcoming social phobias and adopting a confident dating style.

Although it can make dating seem intimidating, social anxiety which may have been a result of prolonged loneliness doesn't have to stop you. Here are some pointers to get over social anxiety and date with confidence:

Understanding Social Fear

I. Determine Triggers: Determine the circumstances (busy areas, first impressions, etc.) that make you anxious when going on dates. Developing coping mechanisms is made possible by this self-awareness.

II. Reject Negative Thoughts: Negative Self-talk is frequently fueled by social anxiety. Realistic affirmations like "I'm interesting" or "I have things to offer" can help counter these ideas.

Increasing Self-Belief

I. Concentrate on Your Strengths: Enumerate your accomplishments, interests, and good traits. Thinking about your advantages increases self-assurance.

II. Big Impact, Small Victories: Begin with casual social encounters that do not involve courting. Engage in conversation with a barista or someone at the gym. Small victories like these boost confidence for larger conversations.

Join a social skills club or work on your conversational abilities with pals. Practice makes progress. You'll get more at ease the more you converse with them.

<u>Strategic Dating Approach</u>

I. Think Beyond Dinners: Make suggestions for conversation-lightening activities, such as going bowling, playing games, or visiting a museum. Experiences that are shared reduce the first uneasiness.

II. Aim to Have a Genuine Conversation with Them: Rather than concentrating on impressing them, try to get to know them better. Make inquiries, pay close attention, and identify shared interests.

III. Accept Humour: Having a little fun can really help. Embrace your inner humor and utilize it as a way to break the ice.

IV. Rejection is Common: Everyone has encountered rejection. Let it go, learn from it, and don't take it personally.

I.   Relaxation Techniques: To reduce your anxiety before a date, try some relaxation exercises like deep breathing or meditation.

II.   Positive Self-Talk: Use self-affirmations frequently to combat pessimistic ideas.

III.   Stay in the Now: Try not to think about the past or hypothetical scenarios. Prioritize learning about your date and savoring the present.

IV.   Turn Around: See the date as a chance to meet new people rather than as a life-or-death circumstance.

Extra Advice

- Put on clothes that give you a sense of self-worth and dress with confidence. It increases your confidence and sense of self-worth.
- Arrive Early: This helps you avoid having to deal with extra anxiety from rushing.
- Stay True to Who You Are: Never try to pass for someone you're not. You will be valued for who you are by the right person.

Recall that having confidence is a journey rather than a destination. Celebrate your accomplishments and exercise self-compassion.

On dates, the majority of people experience some degree of anxiety. You are not by yourself!

Put your attention on enjoying yourself and meeting new people.

You may date with confidence and make lasting relationships by putting these techniques into practice and facing your fears.

Incorporate role-playing activities such as extending an invitation to someone for coffee or enlisting in a new social organization.

Conclusion

In conclusion, one step at a time, building a life you love

Finding a quick fix is not the key to overcoming loneliness; instead, you must set out on a path of self-discovery and create a happy, meaningful life for yourself, whether or not you have a love partner.

This voyage entails:

I.   Embracing vulnerability: Strong friendships and deeper connections are developed when you share your own self with others.

II.   Making self-care a priority: Make an investment in your emotional and physical health by engaging in activities that feed your body, mind, and spirit.

III.   Discovering your passions: Go for interests and pastimes that make you feel accomplished and rekindle your inner flame.

IV.   Creating a solid support network entails taking care of your current relationships, making new ones, and surrounding yourself with positive, encouraging individuals.

Recall that this is an ongoing process. There will be disappointments and times when you doubt yourself, but as you go closer to self-discovery and creating a happy life, you'll feel more confident and purposeful than ever. You'll notice that your sense of loneliness fades as you pursue your passions, take care of yourself, and develop deeper relationships with people. Instead, you'll have a sense of connection and belonging.

So, enjoy the trip. Enjoy every victory, no matter how tiny. and understand that a happy life, full of relationships and significance, is just waiting to be created. This is something you can handle!

Honor Your Triumphs

Recall that this is an ongoing process. There will be disappointments and times when you doubt yourself, but as you go closer to self-discovery and creating a happy life, you'll feel more confident and purposeful than ever.

Never undervalue the importance of monitoring your development! How to do it is as follows:

1. Utilize a diary: Think back on your accomplishments, struggles, and experiences.

2. Make a "wins" list and add points for each time you push yourself beyond your comfort zone, pick up a new skill, or make new friends.

3. Utilise an app progress tracker: To stay motivated, a lot of apps let you establish objectives and graphically monitor your progress.

4. Honour your accomplishments, no matter how tiny! Celebrate your accomplishments and treat yourself as you achieve new heights. This helps

you continue on your journey by reinforcing beneficial behaviours.

You'll notice that your sense of loneliness fades as you pursue your passions, take care of yourself, and develop deeper relationships with people. Instead, you'll have a sense of connection and belonging.

So, enjoy the trip. Enjoy every victory, no matter how tiny. and understand that a happy life, full of relationships and significance, is just waiting to be created. This is something you can handle.

The Dual-Edged Sword of Technology And its Contribution in Spiking Loneliness

The Paradox of Connection

Technology has completely changed how we communicate. Social media platforms facilitate communication with friends and family who live far away, and online forums and groups let us connect with people who share our interests. But loneliness and isolation can equally be exacerbated by the same technologies. Taking a closer look at this two-edged sword and learning how to use it to your advantage for a more satisfying online experience.

The Drawbacks of Interaction

I. Curated Perfection: People's lives are frequently shown on social media as a highlight reel, which raises inflated expectations and feelings of inadequacy.

II. Quantity over Quality: The value of meaningful, face-to-face interactions may be eclipsed by the number of internet contacts.

III.   Cyberbullying and Negativity: The anonymity provided by the internet can encourage nasty speech and cyberbullying.

IV.   The Comparison Trap: Envy and low self-esteem can be stoked by continuously comparing your online persona to that of others.

V.   Screen Time and Social Isolation: Too much screen time can take the place of in-person contact, which can cause a detached and socially isolated feeling.

Using Technology to Advance Humankind

Use social media networks mindfully by being aware of how you use them. Set screen time limits, choose uplifting and motivational content for your feed, and don't be scared to unfollow accounts that undermine your self-esteem.

Look for communities that interest you by using internet platforms. Become a member of online communities, take part in debates, and establish sincere relationships with like-minded individuals.

Don't allow virtual communication to take the place of in-person relationships. Maintain relationships with loved ones through technology, but whenever feasible, give priority to in-person conversations.

It is more satisfying to cultivate a small network of close friends than to amass a big number of virtual acquaintances.

Send thank-you notes to loved ones via technology. Express your gratitude to someone, share a humorous meme, or just be there to listen.

Locating Your Virtual Community

What areas of interest do you have? Try to determine your passions and pastimes first before you decide to look for a community in which your interest fits in. You can probably find an online community for practically anything! Look for social media pages, forums, and discussion groups that are associated with your hobbies.

Avoid being a lurker! Engage in conversation by contributing questions, sharing your own ideas, and sharing your experiences. Online groups that allow you to be authentic and interact with like-minded individuals are the greatest.

Like any other tool, technology can be utilized for good or harm. You may use technology to make your online experience more rewarding and enriching by being aware of its drawbacks and concentrating on using it to create real connections. Instead of isolating yourself with technology, connect with your tribe and create a thriving online community.